THE PRIZE FIGHT

Written By:

MISTY HOLMES DORSEY

DEDICATION

To God my Heavenly Father thank you so much for never giving up on me when I was a complete mess. Words can never express my heart desires for you. Thank you for telling me to write and allowing my writing to continue to bring deliverance in my life.

I would like to dedicate this book to my dad for his time. Thank you for sitting down with me and teaching me the techniques of boxing.

Also to my husband for his love and support. When I was in my worst state you loved me and believed God.

The Prize Fight

CONTENTS

The Prize Fight

ACKNOWLEDGEMENTS

To my Lord and Savior Jesus Christ, for He makes all dreams come true.

To my husband Jeffrey, children Jeffrey Jr., Jessica, to my father Larry Holmes, mother Amelia Bowles for understanding the call of God on my life.

To Elder Marcella Jordan for encouraging me to do all that God has called me to do. To Prophet Maude McCullough for encouraging me to begin to write again and not to let prophetic words that have been spoken over me fall to the ground.

To my cousin Jacqueline Holmes for taking the time to help with the editing process. Thank you for your countless hours.

FORWARDS

Forward by Larry Holmes

Being a world champion means you are the best of the best, the top competitor in your business. Everyone strives to beat you and to take your crown, along with the prestige that accompanies that position. On a daily basis for seven and one-half years, I sacrificed to make sure no one was able to take my title. My new position now allowed me to have the ability to make sure no one in my family every needed to worry about going hungry. In fact, I never went into boxing to become the Heavyweight Champion of the World, but just wanted to make sure my family had enough money for food and rent. Boxing was the avenue that allowed me to care for my mom, brothers and sisters, and later in life, my wife, children and now grandchildren.

A champion has a lot of attributes that are seen in the ring by winning the fight, but there are many distinctions that one must face prior to the night of the fight. Some important factors, besides a healthy diet, are discipline and the will to succeed. To survive in the fight, we must be physically in top shape and mentally ready to defeat our opponents. In everyday life, we will face some form of an opponent who does not want to see you succeed. We are forever jumping over life obstacles that must be confronted and dealt with in a manner that will make you stronger and wiser. It seems like we are always preparing for another confrontation to make us a better human being.

I would like to leave the preaching to my minister-daughter, Misty, but I am a strong believer that, without the faith in

God and yourself, you will never reach your goals in life that will allow you to care for yourself and your family. You must have confidence in yourself before you are able to conquer everyday life and accomplish your goals. I proved all my critics wrong by becoming the Heavyweight Champion of the World. I achieved all of my successes because I believed in myself. One of the best rewards I have ever received was having my children, Misty, Lisa, Belinda, Kandy, and Larry Jr., who I will always cherish and will never stop loving.

Forward By Elder Marcella East Gate Ministries

The Prize Fight by Pastor Misty Dorsey can be described in one word – Deliverance. Pastor Misty Dorsey is the founder and Senior Pastor of Revival Fire Ministries with her husband Pastor Jeffrey Dorsey. Their ministry centers on the prophetic, deliverance, and healing. Pastor Misty's book, The Prize Fight, is an extension of their ministry and can help the reader find the path of true deliverance. She calls it a guide, because it gives insights from the scriptures, her father's (Larry Holmes) fighting expertise and her own life, in a way that illustrates how God is able to set a person free from the enemy's bondage.

Pastor Misty's book is not a theoretical examination of the Word of God, but an explanation of the Word that flows from the wisdom of revealed truth and practical experience. I have witnessed the transformation that God and His Word have created in Pastor Misty's life. As she has applied the Word of God to her life, I watched God transform her from an insecure and suicidal young woman to a powerful prophetic voice in the earth.

The second edition of <u>The Prize Fight</u>, is an expansion of Pastor Misty's original printing and is a "must have" for Pastors, Lay Leaders, or anyone who is struggling or that is helping someone who is struggling to be free of the snare of the enemy.

The Prize Fight

CHAPTER ONE

INTRODUCTION

Whether we believe it or not, we are at war. When you turn on the television, or radio, or log on to the Internet, all you see are images and talk of war.

War is nothing new to the Body of Christ. The period, between Genesis 1:1 and Genesis 1:2, is the time when theologians say Satan was kicked out of heaven. Jesus saw Satan's present and ultimate defeat. [Luke 10:18, Genesis 1:2]

They call this the Gap-Restoration Theory because, according to Genesis 1:1,

In the beginning God created the heaven and the earth.
This informs us that order was established and set in the heavens and earth in the very beginning of creation.

The theory is that chaos (darkness) is now on the scene and God begins to establish order back in the earth.

According to theologians, "Further support is adduced by equating the "the prince of Tyre" in Ezekiel 28 with Satan himself and applying Jeremiah 4:23-26 to a pre-Adamic condition. According to this view, verses 1 and 2 represent the summary of all that the Scriptures reveal of God's original creation, and the following verses are an account of the process of restoration."[1]

This is why they call it the Gap-Restoration Theory.

It is time that we know that, in Christ Jesus, we are victorious and we have already conquered every attack that the enemy will throw our way. He made us *"more than conquerors" (Romans 8:37),* created in His image, walking through time.

Scripture References:

Luke 10:18 - "And he said unto them, I beheld Satan as lightning fall from heaven."

Genesis 1:2 - "And the earth was without form and void; and darkness was upon the face of the deep. And the spirit of God moved upon the face of the waters

---

[1] Samuel J. Schultz, TH.D. Broadening Your Biblical Horizons, Old Testament Survey, Part I: Genesis-Ester, 1964-1968 (Evangelical Training Association),7.

CHAPTER TWO

MY PROCESS

Well, what can I say about my life story at this point since the book is still being written here on the earth. Knowing now that my end will line up with my being as I was in Him (Christ Jesus) and with Him before the foundations of the earth as I stay connected and one with Him.

Well where does one begin in this journey of life? At this point I stop and give a praise break to my Lord that I am still here and able to write and talk about it. Growing up, as the daughter of world famous boxer Larry Holmes would appear to have wonderful benefits especially for someone who was born in Southside Projects of Easton, PA. I had two hard working parents who fought for all they had. I was amongst four siblings and we were always tied to our mother. I struggled to obtain and maintain a place within my daddy's heart after the split of he and my mother. Their separation resulted in an addition of three other siblings being birth that did not grow up with me. Even though, I have seen my dad accomplish a number of feats including becoming rich and famous, I still lived in the shadows somehow. Knowing I was Larry Holmes' first born yet still stuck residing in His shadow and no recognition of who I was because I was still living in the projects and in my rejection.

I can only remember trying to prove and explain to others why I was living in the projects while my rich and famous dad was driving Rolls-Royce's, hanging out with celebrities.

Not realizing or knowing that I have fought for my identity from birth to now. I felt worthless, useless, rejected and ugly. I can remember people calling my dad peanut head and saying I looked like him and how ugly I was. I even recall adults talking in the background about my father and me, even the ones that where supposed to love me.

Having a famous dad many people look at the benefits, but no one really recognizes the stress, struggles and pressure that is put on the children of famous parents. Look at this, Larry Holmes my dad Former World Heavyweight Boxing Champion (WBC) and the International Boxing Federation Champion (IBF), became more of a struggle than a benefit in my life. I am not saying that there where not benefits but for every one of those benefits became a benchmark that I strived on a daily basis to make or keep. People always pulling on you, expecting more from you than anyone else was overwhelming. I had difficulties trying to maintain balance in my life; I had highs and lows. There was no middle ground. It was very difficult for me to find my own identity without being wrapped up in being "Larry Holmes' daughter". It was beneficial to say, "My dad is Larry Holmes", but at the same time an expectation was being created. His name most definitely had a great influence on relationships I formed even in church. I quickly realized there were hidden agendas in ones heart and motivation to draw near to me was not always pure.

At the age of twelve, I accepted Jesus Christ as my personal Savior. However, I never became rooted in the Word of God or learned who I was in Christ. I became a backslider, which began the down-ward spiral of self-destruction. Rooted in false pride, I grew up with low self-esteem and a sense of rejection. This caused much damage to my soul.

As a result of not knowing or believing who I was in Christ I became anorexic and suicidal. The relationships that I formed were codependent relationships.

I was more concerned with taking care of other people than with taking care of me. I continued to give but never received anything in return. I became a people pleaser and did whatever it took for people to like me, even buying my relationships.

I became anorexic and suicidal. The relationships that I formed were codependent relationships. I was more concerned with taking care of other people than with taking care of me. I continued to give but never received anything in return. I became a people pleaser and did whatever it took for people to like me, even buying my relationships.

At the age of 18 I married my wonderful husband Jeffrey Dorsey. He encouraged me and I began to see that it was possible to have a future. We wanted the marriage to take place in the church where we grew up. However, neither one of us attended church regularly. In order to get married in the church, we were required to attend services and participate in pre-marital counseling sessions.

Therefore, this was the only reason that we went to church. During a Sunday service, Pastor Juanita Davis was preaching with such power and force. After her sermon, I was led by the Holy Spirit to give my life back to Christ. At that point, I became serious about my commitment to Christ.

Shortly after being married we were blessed with two wonderful children, Jeffrey, Jr. and Jessica. However, I still had low self-esteem and I was still suicidal. Even though I had a husband who truly loved me and two beautiful children who I adored, I wasn't capable of loving myself. I began to read the Bible, attend Tuesday afternoon prayer services and Wednesday night Prayer and Bible Study. I became empowered by the Word of God and began to fight for my life.

At the age of twenty-six, I had a TIA, which is a slight stroke. This left me with little use of my right side. However, God is a true healer because He has healed my body and restored all my limbs. My extremities now function at one hundred percent. Realize, I heard what the doctors had said to me, but by this time The Word of God was in me to the point that I did not receive anything at this point, but I was already healed.

I was still struggling with my life and had many ups and downs that I needed some help. Therefore, my doctor prescribed Prozac for me to help maintain a balance, but instead, it left me feeling lethargic. I realized I wasn't laughing and enjoying myself anymore; this was a part of me that I liked. Then one day, the Lord spoke to me and said that He had healed me. After God spoke this to me, I shared this with those who were close to me. I also stopped taking the Prozac, along with beta? blocker for my heart. I obeyed God, but it was still recommended that I should see my doctors. I decided that, if the doctors saw no improvement, I would go back on the medicine. After visiting all of my doctors and taking various tests, I was informed that they were discontinuing my medications. I had been healed, delivered, and set free by the power and blood of Jesus Christ.

When I accepted Christ in my life, I began to experience many changes in my life. I began to have hope and saw an expected end, with a great expectation, with Christ Jesus in my life. No longer would I try to cut my wrists, take an overdose, or lie in the middle of a street, expecting a car to run me over. I saw hope and a glorious future in my Savior. I began to see myself as somebody made in the image of God.

My covenant sisters helped me as I began my Christian journey. They had me rehearse who I was in Christ daily. I learned how to form new pathways and abort old roads that led to self-destruction. I was able to listen to positive things said about me, without rejecting them, and learned to reject negative things that were contrary to the Word of God. [Romans 12:1-2, Philippians 2:5]

I realized that I had to begin to live my new life and allow the old man to be crucified with Christ. I had to **let** the mind of Christ get in me. I had a choice and I was going to do whatever it took. I began to learn how to discipline myself to be the disciple that Christ wanted me to be. I am still striving to be what He has predestined me to be.[2 Corinthians 5:17, Galatians 2:20, I Corinthians 9:24-27]

Every morning, afternoon and evening, I would go to a mirror and look at myself. I would remind myself who I was in Christ Jesus until it became a part of me. I would display different Scriptures, which are the promises of God, on the dashboard of my cars. I would put my name in front of the Scripture and rehearse it until it became a part of me; until my mind began to be renewed. This gave me power by knowing who I was, and that nothing could take it away from me. I learned how to fight against my mind and put the carnal mind in subjection to the Spirit of God. I learned how to say STOP and renew my thinking according to the Word of God. [Romans 8:7]

I remember reading a book by Morris Cerrello and one passage stated that, "Whoever controls the mind of men controls that man." I was determined, after reading that passage; only God was going to control my mind.

I'm not telling you that it was easy, but by rehearsing and living the Word of God, God can and will change your mindset. I learned to set my mind on things above. I also reminded myself that I am already sitting in heavenly places in Christ Jesus.

By not knowing who I am, I have come face to face with many battles in my life and gave the enemy access to me by making decisions in my life that were contrary to the Word of God. Thanks be to God, today I have no doubt, and I have the confidence that I can stand strong and say who I am, and that no devil can tell me anything different. I had become passionate and violent when it came to the things of God and realized that I am a force to reckon with because the Greater One lives in me. [Matthew 11:12]

Today, I can truly say old things have passed away and behold all things have become new. I am a new creature and have been empowered by the Holy Spirit to awaken, arise, spring forth, go forth and do all that he has put into my hands. Today I am a wife, mother of three, and grandmother of seven. I have answered the prophetic call on my life to go into the world and preach the Gospel of Jesus as well as to root out, to pull down, and to destroy, to throw down, to build, and to plant. God has strengthen me beyond my limits and has called me to preach truth whether they hear or whether they forebear. Today I oversee churches, pastor, prophecy, evangelize and teach where He sends me. I raise, train, and set forth prophets into the nations. For I am a bond servant of the Lord Jesus Christ.

Scripture References:

Romans 12:1-2 - *"I beseech you therefore, brethren, by the mercies of God, that ye present your bodies a living sacrifice, holy, acceptable unto God, which is your reasonable service. And be not conformed to this world: but be ye transformed* by the renewing of your mind, that ye may prove what is that good, and acceptable, and perfect, will of God."

Philippians 2:5 - "Let this mind be in you, which was also in Christ Jesus:"

2 Corinthians 5;17 - "Therefore if any man be in Christ, he is a new creature: old things are passed away; behold all things are become new."

Galatians 2:20 - "I am crucified with Christ: nevertheless I live; yet not I, but Christ liveth in me: and the life which I now live in the flesh I live by the faith of the Son of God, who loved me, and gave himself for me."

1 Corinthians 9:24-27 (NIV) - "Do you not know that in a race all the runners run, but only one gets the prize? Run in such a way as to get the prize. Everyone who competes in the games goes into strict training. They do it to get a crown that will not last, but we do it to get a crown that will last forever. Therefore I do not run like someone running aimlessly; I do not fight like a boxer beating the air. No, I strike a blow to my body and make it my slave so that after I have preached to others, I myself will not be disqualified for the prize."

Romans 8:7 - "Because the carnal mind is enmity against God: for it is not subject to the law of God, neither indeed can be.

Matthew 11:12 - "And from the days of John the Baptist until now the kingdom of heaven suffereth violence, and the violent take it by force

"Violent - bee-as-tace'; Strong's G973 - from G971; a forcer, that is, (figuratively) energetic: - violent."[2]

---

[2] James Strong, LL.D.,S.T.D. The New Strong's Exhaustive Concordance of the Bible, 1822-1894, Thomas Nelson Publishers, 1990.

1 John 4:4 - "Ye are of God, little children, and have overcome them: because greater is he that is in you, than he that is in the world."

Romans 8:37 - "Nay, in all these things we are more than conquerors through him that loved us"

Song of Solomon 6:3 - "I am my beloved's, and my beloved is mine: he feedeth among the lilies."

CHAPTER THREE

GOD HAS NOT GIVEN US
THE SPIRIT OF FEAR

Fear is a Spirit and it wants to paralyze you from becoming all that God has purposed in your life. Fear wants to face you on a daily basis and wants to take you out. It is a spirit that presents itself powerful and will have you self destruct without the enemy exerting much energy. Fear is not an emotion it is a Spirit that has motives and is determined to keep you in bondage. One of the purposes of fear is to blind you from the truth. Fear is designed to keep you focused on past failures, rejections and disappointments and force you to go into the bedroom get in the bed and prevent you from moving. Fear will dry up the waters and cause the spirit of depression to leap on you. [I Timothy 1:7, I John 4:17-18]

One thing we must come to realize is that when we mature in God's love fear is dealt with. Fear is violently cast to the ground. Fear is removed from off of your shoulders and is destroyed because the anointing that is being released through us. Fear is crushed and every bit of fight or retaliation that lies in fear is destroyed when love becomes perfected in us. When our love matures in Christ we come to know that Christ is our Head and He is the Head of all things. Fear is defeated and the power of fear is destroyed in Christ Jesus. Do not let fear keep you running. Also, do not allow fear to disqualify you from receiving the blessings of the Lord.

Make a solid decision today that fear will not have permission to dry up your waters. Remember Christ promises to be in him a well of living water. Our waters should never run dry or become stagnant. [John 4:14]

Realize that the battle with fear has been won. Christ has conquered death, hell and the grave and is seated on the right hand of the Father praying for us. When we come to the place and realize the **love** and **power** that God has given us from the beginning we can truly operate in un-measurable anointing. The love of Christ has poured out on Calvary for us. The sound of mind that Christ has made available to us. When our eyes open we come to understand with limit vocabulary what an **Awesome God** we serve and what a powerful people we are, when we accepted Jesus as Lord and Savior of our lives. There is nothing that the devil can do to or try to do that the Word of God cannot deliver us from. We are only alive, I mean living the abundant life that Christ has promised us before Christ destroyed the works of the enemy. The enemy's works have already been destroyed. We need to grab a hold of this truth. Understand, when we are his disciples truth is released in us and brings us to a place of freedom.

Fear wants to be present to stop the plan that God has for your life. Fear wants you to be a lethargic and an unproductive Christian that has not tapped into their full potential. [John 8:31-32]

Truth has an assignment if you are disciples of God. It must bring the Saints of God into a place of freedom. The Word of God says it will make you free. If you are a disciple you have no choice in the matter truth will come to you when you're not looking for it; because it must deliver you out of your own flesh and out of the hands of the enemy. Many tell God what they want Him to touch and what not to touch. I got some good news if you are a disciple truth is coming after those things that wants us to remain fearful, blinded and unproductive. Truth comes to bring deliverance.

We cannot fight Satan or his fallen angels on our own. Psalms 8:5 tell us that we were made a little lower than the angels. We need God's strength.

"Finally, brethren (not just an individual but the Body of Christ), be strong in the Lord (Adonai =Master, Ruler), and in the power of his might." Ephesians 6:10

"Power (kratos) – Dominion, strength, manifested power. Signifies exerted strength, power shown effectively in a reigning authority."[3]

We cannot successfully do battle with the devil unless the strength we need comes from God. According to Tony Evans, "Many of us tend to swing toward one of two extremes when it comes to the devil.

- Some overestimate him. They become fearful and timid, lest Satan leap upon them. [I John 4:4]

---

[3] J Jack W. Hayford, Litt.D., Bishop Ithiel C. Clemmons, M.Div.,Ph.D.,D.D., Spirit Filled Life Bible (KJV), 1991, 1995, Thomas Nelson Publishers.

- Others underestimate the devil. Yes, Satan is a defeated foe. But even though he is nothing more than a condemned death row inmate awaiting execution, it is not wise to sleep in his cell."[4]

When we overestimate Satan, he sees our fears and our weakness, and jumps right on us.

We are going to fight one way or another. Even when we stand still and see the salvation of the Lord is a form of fighting, but fighting from a different position.

When God created us he gave us dominion and authority. [Genesis 1:28]

Scripture References:

*1 Timothy 1:7 - "For God hath not given us the spirit of fear; but of **power**, and of **love** and of a **sound mind.**"*

1 John 4:17-18 - "Herein is our love made perfect, that we may have boldness in the day of judgment: because as he is, so are we in this world. There is no fear in love; but perfect love casteth out fear: because fear hath torment. He that feareth is not made perfect in love."

John 4:14 - "But whosoever drinketh of the water that I shall give him shall never thirst; but the water that I shall give him shall be in him a well of water springing up into everlasting life."

---

[4] Anthony T. Evans, Th.d, Winning the Invisible Battle, 1991, The Urban Alternative, Inc., 4.

John 8:31-32 - "Then said Jesus to those Jews which believed on him, If ye continue in my word, then are ye my disciples indeed; And ye shall know the truth, and the **truth shall make you free.***"*

1 John 4:4 "Ye are of God, little children, and have overcome them: because greater is he that is in you, than he that is in the world"

Genesis 1:28 - "And God blessed them, and God said unto them, Be fruitful, and multiply, and replenish the earth, and subdue it: and have dominion over the fish of the sea, and over the fowl of the air, and over every living thing that moveth upon the earth."

CHAPTER FOUR

KNOWING YOUR PURPOSE

When one prepares for battle, he/she needs to know who they are in Christ, what They have in Christ, and what they can do in Christ. [Romans 12:2]

Be strong in the Lord. We need to trust, rely and depend on God. Be disciplined saints. This means we need to pray, fast, read the Word of God, meditate on the goodness and character of God, praise, worship, witness, and testify to others.

Many people go through life trying to find their purpose. They look in many arenas trying to find one's purpose. However, true purpose can only be found in Christ Jesus who is the Head all. Only God can give you the meaning of purpose. The world will never actually be able to define what your true purpose and your true calling is.

As saints of God when we do not know who we are, and why God created us a demonic door has the potential of opening up and giving the enemy access to us. We then have the potential of becoming dangerous to ourselves and to others. When I say a demonic door I am talking about a door that we opened and Satan walked right in. Every decision that we make must be based on the Word. We cannot and must not get caught up in our emotions and allow the enemy legal access to us. Without God there is no way of knowing your true purpose. Those without Christ think after a certain age they are done, but with God purpose remains. You are not done because you may have retired in the natural with God purpose continue throughout your entire life. In God we do not retire. The only way to find purpose is finding God and developing a relationship with Him and His Son and allowing the Holy Spirit to have its perfect work in you revealing the will of the Father. [Genesis 4:1-7]

"Purpose is:

1. the reason for which something exists or is done, made, used, etc.

2. an intended or desired result; end; aim; goal.

3. determination; resoluteness.

4. the subject in hand; the point at issue.

5. practical result, effect, or advantage: to act to good purpose."[5]

"Purpose – prosthesis - *proth'-es-is*; Strong's G4286; from G4388; a *setting forth*, that is, (figuratively) *proposal*

[5] Purpose. (n.d.). *Dictionary.com Unabridged.* Retrieved September 26, 2011, from Dictionary.com website:
http://dictionary.reference.com/browse/purpose

(*intention*); specifically the *show* bread (in the Temple) as *exposed* before God: - purpose, shew [-bread]."[6]

When one knows their purpose it will sustain them. God will sustain us when we know our purpose, and choose to walk out our purpose in our obedience to God. Remember purpose bring us into presence with an Almighty God. When one is in the presence of God one cannot escape purpose because God's presence has us face our purpose. A God who knows all about you and what He has predestined for you.

When looking up purpose it is amazing to see one of the Greek words that describe purpose is showbread. The shewbread was also known as the "bread of the presence".
We are His royal priesthood and as priests we have the right to the shewbread.

The shewbread was only eaten by the priest. The priest ate the bread in the Holy Place, because there portion was in the holy place. Realize Saints our portion is in His presence. [Exodus 25:30] We are the priest of God [1 Peter 2:9]

God desire for man is to enter into His presence and have fellowship with Him. Jesus had clear understanding what His purpose was because He was in constant fellowship with the Father who revealed His will to Christ Jesus. I have come to understand that we must thrash out our issues and submit to God. Wrestle those things to the ground and do not allow them to interfere with what God has purposed in our life. [Matthew 26:42, John 6:35, John 6:49-50]

I have come to understand through a powerful Woman of God,

---

[6] Purpose. (1995). In *Strong's exhaustive concordance: King James.* (Updated ed.). Retrieved September 26, 2011, from http://www.biblestudytools.com/concordances/strongs- exhaustive-concordance/

Elder Marcella Jordan of East Gate Ministries that if you do not call things the way God calls them you will never move into your purpose. She shared with us on a Monday Night Healing Service that God never called it manna he called it bread. Moses called it bread. However, the people called it manna meaning "what is this."

Again, when God reveals your purpose to you one must call it the way God calls it. Do not change what God has spoken to you because it does not look familiar to you. Jesus said,

"I am the bread of life. He who comes to me will never go hungry, and he who believes in me will never be thirsty. ... Your forefathers ate the manna in the desert, yet they died. But here is the bread that comes down from heaven, which a man may eat and not die." John 6:35, 49-50

If you choose to eat your "what" it will not sustain you. Call it what God calls it. Bread! Even when it looks unfamiliar. How many times has God given us something to sustain us and we called it "what". Change your language. [Leviticus 24:5-9]

The Word of God is full with purpose, destiny and a road plan and guidelines to aid you in becoming all that God has purposed and will help you to get where God is calling you and will teach you how to stand in what God is saying.

When one does not know their purpose and how to get there; anyone can tell him anything and any road can lead you there. It is vital key to know that God is faithful to His purpose and He has already gone before you. Therefore, if you follow Him you will never end up in the place called nowhere. [Psalms 37:23, Psalms 119:105]

God wants all his creation to understand what their purpose is and walk in it. When He created man God told them what their purpose was. God is not a God that will try to confuse you and keep you guessing. He wants you to come to Him and allow Him to talk to you while you listen and receive the plan that He has laid out for our lives. He is not a God that will lie about your purpose and not fulfill what He has called you to. God is not a man, that He should lie.

God wants purpose fulfilled in our lives that the mistakes that we make when we take wrong turns He allows those turns to work out for our good. They are learning experience teaching us how to train our ears to hear accurately. [Genesis 1:26, Numbers 23:19]

Victory will be looking him straight in his face when he realizes why God created him . Knowing your purpose and walking it out in the Spirit will arm you with the artillery to take out any enemy that comes up to you. You will be able to identify it is the enemy and his message. You will come to know that what he is bringing is a direct counterfeit to what God has decreed and declared over you.

Remember what God said it will not return unto him void. Understand something, man's words falls to the ground, but God Words never, no never falls to the ground. So what God has spoken over you and determined what you were to do is always on assignment to bring God's plan to pass that God will get the glory. [Isaiah 55:10-12]

When talking with my dad, one thing he told me over and over is that when he realized who he was and what was in him; he became determined to become what he saw. He was going to do what was necessary to discipline his flesh so he would be able to achieve what he saw. He had people around him that did not agree with what he declared out of his mouth. Many negative comments came at him but he did not lose what he saw. They told him that he would never be the WBC Heavyweight Boxing Champ because he was too small. When he got older they told him that nothing was in him all was gone; they told him that he was over the hill.

I remember one magazine saying to him holding my son in his arms can this grandpa do it. He proved them wrong. I never meet a man that was so disciplined. Because of his training and wanting to stay focused he missed out on many of my school events that I wished he was present for. However, he always told us (his children) I am doing this for you. You need to grab hold of something. My dad had made up in his mind that he was going to give his children some type of security .

I thank my Heavenly Father today, because He made it all possible by sending His only begotten Son into this world for us. Jesus who was in constant fellowship with the Father comes to earth with a purpose to purchase was back to God by and through His blood. That we would be reconciled and be heirs and joint heirs to the promise. I thank you Jesus for giving your children your Bride the ultimate security. The only security that can guarantee eternal life.

Sometimes, we as Saints forget to grab hold of those Scriptures that show us the ultimate love and sacrifice. [John 3:16)

I realize now, but not back then, that my dad was pursuing his purpose. Many times it felt that his love was far away. Now, I have come to see that His love was always present trying to make a better life for us than the one he grew up in.

In ministry I have come to realize that there are sacrifices that one will make and walk through. There is a cost when one pursues real ministry. My dad only wanted to stay focused. He did not want anything to catch him off guard, because he had purpose steering him in his face. When one is purposed their timeline may be different from those around them. There is a choice that one must make and be disciplined not to allow your surroundings to affect your choice. This has caused many fighters to get knocked out, distracted and throw punches that never connected. Also, fighters have lost their lives because they did not know how to stay focused on what was before them.

There were those that just did not see what was inside of my dad. However, he was able to see something in himself that others could not and would not recognize. They basically told him to be glad and content with just being a sparring partner for Mohammad Ali and should not think about becoming champ. He had a motto, when they say I can't that when I can. He became like the little engine that said, "I think I can, I think I can" then changed his speech to, "I can."

When one is determined because they have set their eyes on God to move beyond hindrances and circumstances nothing can stop them. The enemy will try but the discipline they have walked in has caused them not to respond to the enemy tactics. They have now learned how to move forward to achieve the promises that was purposed in one's life. Priorities may seem out of order but they are not to the individual. It was never that my dad did not love us, but there was an unction in him telling him to stay focused and never get caught off guard. I am not saying that he was a bad dad, but I am saying when he was not training we had much time and time that was full of purpose. When he was training he was focused and he did not allow anything to throw him off guard. He took care of things at home and the businesses before he left for camp. He also had people in place that he could trust to run his businesses. Wow, how many things did we allow to come and distract us from purpose. Although married for over 25 years he would not allow intimacy with his wife to throw him off because he understood that his strength to fight was important. If an individual in the natural can stay focused to walk out his purpose. Why do we in the Body of Christ struggle so much with our flesh. Our flesh is not to dictate to us we are to dictate to it.

Two Scriptures that holds so true to me and I grab hold of them and repeat them as often as I can. They are constantly releasing sanity in me. I realize when I do not rehearse these Scripture warfare gets greater and there is a struggle for me to hold on to what God has said to me concerning purpose. These Scriptures are powerful Scriptures that when they get activated the radical love for God and a heart to obey God is released inside me; that take fighter in me begins to take it by force. [Matthew 11:12]

Once the Word is active nothing can stop the **Word** or you from doing what the Word has decreed over you and through you. The Word gets activated by you declaring out of your own mouth. I am not talking about someone declaring the Word out of their mouth; nor am I minimizing the power of the Word that God speaks out of others mouths. But something happens when you open up your mouth and begin to decree and to declare. When the Word comes out of you, the Word will release insight and revelation. You will begin to see what you thought was impossible now is possible. The Word becomes personal. When the Word comes out of your own mouth and penetrates your inner ear and open up your eyeball (prophetically) you can see and discern the things of God, your mindset will change. I am telling you Word will transform your mind and your mindset. We now will have the mindset of God. [Hebrews 4:12]

This is due to the fact that the Word of God is able to reveal and discern all (person, place or thing). The Word of God will expose anything that is in you or in the workings to destroy

the plan of God for your life. It makes all things naked.
[Hebrews 4:13]

What I am saying your old mind is no longer present because
you are now walking in the mind of Christ. Old things have
been passed away, all things are become new [II Corinthians
5:17]. Do not allow the enemy to keep you from speaking the
Word of God. I do not care how you feel. Word brings life to
every dry and dead area in your life. It was the Word that
resurrected Lazarus from the dead. [John 11:43]

When the Word is spoken purpose is released. Word on
assignment to bring the Word in existence. It is so.

Realize what God has purposed for your life. When your
mouth begins to confess the Word of God confession is made
unto salvation. Understand there is more to salvation than
we think, we cannot just stop at accepting Jesus Christ we
must allow salvation to have its perfect work in us. [Romans
10:1]

*"For with the heart man believeth unto righteousness; and
with the mouth confession is made unto salvation."*
Romans 10:1

"Salvation - sōtēria - *so-tay-ree'-ah; Strong's* G4991;
feminine of a derivative of G4990 as (properly abstract)
noun; *rescue* or *safety* (physically or morally): - deliver,
health, salvation, save, saving."[7]

---

[7] Jack W. Hayford, Litt.D., Bishop Ithiel C. Clemmons,
M.Div.,Ph.D.,D.D.,
Spirit Filled Life Bible (KJV), 1991, 1995, Thomas Nelson Publishers.

Salvation is to rescue us and keep us in the state where the Word of God has access to us to keep on delivering us from ourselves when the carnal man refuses to die. It is to keep us in a healthy state in our spirit, soul and body. Bringing every part of us in subjection to the Spirit of God.

Now the fighter gets released to slay and take back what the enemy has stolen and is trying to steal from you. The Word gets so activated inside of you that it assures and confirms that nothing is out of reach for those that are in Christ Jesus. These Scriptures will make what looks impossible become possible. [Matthew 19:26]

The Word will set you free from the chains of bondage of self and man's opinions about you. [Psalms 56:4, Psalms 118:6, Hebrews 13;6]

Many will see that the God you serve as LORD GOD. They will come to know that your God is the BIG GOD, and that He is.

Those Scriptures are:

> *"Ye are of God, little children, and have overcome them: because greater is he that is in you, than he that is in the world. They are of the world: therefore speak they of the world, and the world heareth them. We are of God: he that knoweth God heareth us; he that is not of God heareth not us. Hereby know we the spirit of truth, and the spirit of error." 1 John 4:4-6*

> *"I can do all things through Christ which strengtheneth me." Philippians 4:13*

These Scriptures will fight the carnal man. They will land a powerful left jab followed by a powerful right hand that will

knock the enemy out; then cause you to go for the head. Don't leave the head on the enemy.
When the enemy is down you must take off his head.
Goliaths and the tormentors, once the Word has knocked them out keep speaking the Word and allow Sword of the Spirit which is the Word cut the head of the enemy off.

Realize our battle is not against flesh and blood. Therefore we do not war after the flesh. The Word of God knocks them out and the Sword of the Lord is executed and slays them so your purpose is accomplished without hindrances. These scriptures will push all doubts, reasoning and negativity out of you. God will become so enormous, big, and massive in you that the enemy or anyone that cannot believe what God has said, they will only be a witness watching God fulfill His purpose in my life.

Let me tell you, God created me with a purpose. Just like He created you with purpose. I am a warrior for God. It's in my blood. Growing up, I did not understand my purpose, but as I walk with God, He continues to show more and more of my purpose each day.   Having a dad who is a boxer, I now understand my purpose is to stand in the gap for people and fight for people and fight until the promises of God are established in and on the earth. [Matthew 6:10]

Scripture References:

Romans 12:2 -"And be not conformed to this world: but be ye transformed by the renewing of your mind, and that ye may prove what is that good, and acceptable, and perfect will of God."

Genesis 4:1-7 - "And Adam knew Eve his wife; and she conceived, and bare Cain, and said, I have gotten a man from the LORD. And she again bare his brother Abel. And Abel was a keeper of sheep, but Cain was a tiller of the ground. And in process of time it came to pass, that Cain brought of the fruit of the ground an offering unto the LORD. And Abel, he also brought of the firstlings of his flock and of the fat thereof. And the LORD had respect unto Abel and to his offering: But unto Cain and to his offering he had not respect. And Cain was very wroth, and his countenance fell. And the LORD said unto Cain, Why art thou wroth? and why is thy countenance fallen? If thou doest well, shalt thou not be accepted? and if thou doest not well, sin lieth at the door. And unto thee shall be his desire, and thou shalt rule over him."

Exodus 25:30 (ESV) - "And you shall set the bread of the Presence on the table before me regularly."

1 Peter 2:9 - "But ye are a chosen generation, a royal priesthood, an holy nation, a peculiar people; that ye should shew forth the praises of him who hath called you out of darkness into his marvellous light:"

Matthew 26:42 - "He went away again the second time, and prayed, saying, O my Father, if this cup may not pass away from me, except I drink it, thy will be done."

John 6:35 - "And Jesus said unto them, I am the bread of life: he that cometh to me shall never hunger; and he that believeth on me shall never thirst."

John 6:49-50 - "Your fathers did eat manna in the wilderness, and are dead. This is the bread which cometh down from heaven, that a man may eat thereof, and not die."

Leviticus 24:5-9 - "And thou shalt take fine flour, and bake twelve cakes thereof: two tenth deals shall be in one cake. And thou shalt set them in two rows, six on a row, upon the pure table before the LORD. And thou shalt put pure frankincense upon each row, that it may be on the bread for a memorial, even an offering made by fire unto the LORD. Every sabbath he shall set it in order before the LORD continually, being taken from the children of Israel by an everlasting covenant. And it shall be Aaron's and his sons'; and they shall eat it in the holy place: for it is most holy unto him of the offerings of the LORD made by fire by a perpetual statute."

Psalms 37:23 - "The steps of a good man are ordered by the LORD: and he delighteth in his way."

Psalms 119:105 - "NUN. Thy word is a lamp unto my feet, and a light unto my path."

Genesis 1:26 - "And God said, Let us make man in our image, after our likeness: and let them have dominion over the fish of the sea, and over the fowl of the air, and over the cattle, and over all the earth, and over every creeping thing that creepeth upon the earth."

Numbers 23:19 - "God is not a man, that he should lie; neither the son of man, that he should repent: hath he said, and shall he not do it? or hath he spoken, and shall he not make it good?"

Isaiah 55:10-12 - "For as the rain cometh down, and the snow from heaven, and returneth not thither, but watereth the earth, and maketh it bring forth and bud, that it may give seed to the sower, and bread to the eater: So shall my word be that goeth forth out of my mouth: it shall not return unto me void, but it shall accomplish that which I please, and it shall prosper in the thing whereto I sent it. For ye shall go out with joy, and be led forth with peace: the mountains and the hills shall break forth before you into singing, and all the trees of the field shall clap their hands."

John 3:16 - "For God so loved the world, that he gave his only begotten Son, that whosoever believeth in him should not perish, but have everlasting life."

Matthew 11:12 - "And from the days of John the Baptist until now the kingdom of heaven suffereth violence, and the violent take it by force."

Hebrews 4:12 - "For the word of God is quick, and powerful, and sharper than any twoedged sword, piercing even to the dividing asunder of soul and spirit, and of the joints and marrow, and is a discerner of the thoughts and intents of the heart."

Hebrews 4:13 - Neither is there any creature that is not manifest in his sight: but all things are naked and opened unto the eyes of him with whom we have to do.

John 11:43 - "And when he thus had spoken, he cried with a loud voice, Lazarus, come forth".

Matthew 19:25 - "But Jesus beheld them, and said unto them, With men this is impossible; but with God all things are possible."

Psalms 56:4 - "In God I will praise his word, in God I have put my trust; I will not fear what flesh can do unto me."

Psalms 118:6 - "The LORD is on my side; I will not fear: what can man do unto me?"

Hebrews 13:6 - "So that we may boldly say, The Lord is my helper, and I will not fear what man shall do unto me"

Matthew 6:10 - "Thy kingdom come. Thy will be done in earth, as it is in heaven."

CHAPTER FIVE

ATTITUDE FOR WAREFARE

When you prepare for warfare, you must understand that a certain attitude comes along with the attire.

I sat down with my dad about 2 years ago and began to ask him to tell me everything he does to prepare for a fight. The first thing he said to me was, "You need to be disciplined. You can't do what you want to do; you can't eat what you want to eat; and you can't go anywhere you want to go." Basically, he was saying your life is not your own. [I Corinthians 9:27]

• You must become serious about what you are doing.

My dad said, "When I didn't have a fight coming up, I wasn't serious." He would train but his training was not as focused as it was when he was preparing for a fight. On some days, he trained and on some days if he did not feel like it, he did not train.

As the Body of Christ, we need to be serious about the things of God at all times. We are in a war every day, not just some days. Satan's assignment is to kill you; he wants you dead. He knows one will put a thousand to flight and two will put ten thousand to flight. He wants you out of the way. You would become one less witness in the world, witnessing for Christ.

We cannot afford not to pick up our Bibles every day, and read and study them. The Word of God is the bread for our bodies. The Word of God will condition us to be ready for whatever comes our way. We cannot afford to go without the Word any day in our life.

When we don't feel like reading the Word of God, we need to read it. We need to condition our Spirit to dictate to our soul and our soul to dictate to our body, not our flesh dictating to our spirit. [Luke 1:46-47]

Once your Spirit has received, then your soul can rejoice, and your members of your body can express what your Spirit has already received.

Scripture References:

1 Corinthians 9:27 - But I keep under my body, and bring it into subjection: lest that by any means, when I have preached to others, I myself should be a castaway.

Luke 1:46-47 - "And Mary said, My soul doth (action, currently happening) magnify the Lord, And my spirit hath (past tense) rejoiced in God my Saviour."

CHAPTER SIX

PREPARING FOR WARFARE

- Watch what you feed your body (your temple).

My dad also said that when he was preparing for a fight, he could not eat what he wanted to eat. If he wanted a Whopper, he could not eat it because the grease was not good for his body.

I Corinthians 3:16 –17 - "Know ye not that ye are the temple of God, and that the spirit dwelleth in you. If any man defile the temple of God, him shall God destroy; for the temple of God is holy, which temple ye are."

Many people just stop at verse 16, but you need to read verse 17 as well. We can't take and put anything in this temple and expect God to bless it. The temple is the place where Christ dwells.

Let me ask you a question that the Holy Spirit asked me.

- Where do you take your temple?
- What is your temple taking in?
- Is it edifying? Is it building you up and the Body of Christ up?

If it is not building you and the Body of Christ up, then we need to check it. God is a Holy God.

- You have got to get the proper amount of sleep and you need to get the right sleep.

We need the Shalom of God, which is the Peace of God. Many people sleep but their minds is running all night long, and when they get up, they are tired.

- You have got to get up early in the morning to workout. [Psalms 63:1]

My dad told me that he gets up and he thinks "I got to fight, I got to fight, and I got to fight." He begins to speak to himself.

- You need to prepare your mind.

He gets up every day and reminds himself that he is Larry Holmes, The Champ. We must get up and remind ourselves who we are and declare who we are with our lips saying, "We are sons of God." [1 John 3:2, Philippians 2:5]

- He said, "You can't hang out with everybody, Misty. I cannot hang out with negative folks, people who are not going anywhere; have no vision and cannot see where I am going. I cannot be around them; I have got to cut them off. If they cannot support who I am, then they've got to go."

I can remember this and it still is happening today. When they see my dad, they still call him Champ, even though he may not hold the title. I used to wonder, "Why do they call him the Champ, and not Larry?" Which is his first name. I have come to realize that they see him as the Champ.

He also said that negative people would bring you down with all of their negativity. Sharing your vision prematurely can lead you to the pit, just like Joseph (Genesis 37). God has spoken things over our lives and, if we share them with people and they can't receive it, we may need to examine our relationships to see if they are a positive influence in our life. Remember, that when you share your vision with others, be led by God.

We need to make a decision that we are not going to allow anyone to keep us from walking in the things that God has ordained for us. God is a powerful God, and we, in Christ, are a powerful people. Don't settle for being an ordinary person because the God you serve is not an ordinary God.

- You need to think on positive things. [Philippians 4:8]

- You need to work out in the afternoon or evening as well. [Psalms 55:17]

There are times that my dad goes to the gym when no one is around. You do not need to let everyone know what you are doing. Sometimes, when he works out in the evenings, spectators are present. They are watching, observing and learning his techniques.

One day, I brought one of my professors from college to watch my dad train. My professor brought people with him and they brought their camcorders to film my dad. My uncle immediately came to stop them from filming. I explained who they were, but he didn't seem to care. He

47

explained to me that people from the outside come to the gym to spy. They observe the various techniques and strategies, and report their observations back to their camps. This enables the opponent to learn how to be prepared and how to defend themselves against the battle that they are about to face.

- You need to shadow box, which is a boxing technique where you watch yourself in a mirror. You can see your style, your strategies and your timing. The idea is to try to avoid hitting yourself in the mirror. This technique will make you aware of how to fight defensively. It also teaches you how to land a jab and move.

- The heavy bag workout is just what it sounds like: a workout. It builds your body up and puts you up against heavy weight. When you swing the bag around, you have to realize that the bag is going to come back at you with its full weight and force. Two things happen when you work with the heavy bag: 1) your upper body is being strengthened and 2) your hitting power is being increased.

Realize that when Satan comes, he is not coming empty-handed. He has a bag of tricks that he is ready to throw at you. When you think he is finished, he comes with something else. Sometimes, he just throws it at you all at once, without giving you a chance to regroup. [Jude 1:20]

- The speed bag is a bag that comes back at you quickly without giving you a chance to respond. When you hit that bag, it swings back, hits the board and then comes back at you. If you are not alert and quick, you will not be able to block the blows coming your way. This also helps with your timing, rhythm and quickness. You cannot hit the bag once and expect to improve your timing. [Ecclesiastes 3:1]

- My dad also talked about working out for 6 days and resting on the 7th

We, the body of Christ, need to learn how to take time and just rest in the presence of an Almighty God. We need to allow the Father's refreshing, restoring, renewing, and reviving power to minister to us as we rest in His presence. [Isaiah 40:31]

Scripture References:

Psalms 63:1 - "O God, thou art my God; early will] seek thee; my soul thirsteth for thee, my flesh longeth for thee in a dry and thirsty land, where no water is."

1 John 3:2 - "Beloved, now are we the sons of God, and it doth not yet appear what we shall be: but we know that, when he shall appear, we shall be like him, for we shall see him as he is."

Philippians 2:5 - "Let this mind be in you, which was also in Christ Jesus."

Philippians 4:8 - "Finally brethren whatsoever things are true, whatsoever things are honest, whatsoever things are just, whatsoever things are pure, whatsoever things that are lovely, whatsoever things are good report; if there be any virtue, and if there be any praise, think on these things."

Psalms 55:17 - "Evening, and morning, and at noon, will I pray, and cry aloud; and he shall hear my voice."

Jude 1:20 - "But ye, beloved, building up yourselves on your most holy faith, praying in the Holy Ghost",

Ecclesiastes 3:1 - To every thing there is a season, and a time to every purpose under the heaven:

Isaiah 40:31 - "But they that wait upon the LORD shall renew their strength; they shall mount up with wings as eagles; they shall run, and not be weary; and they shall walk, and not faint."

CHAPTER SEVEN

KNOWING YOUR OPPONENT

Every fight that comes your way is not yours. You need to choose your battles. There are certain battles that God has ordained for you. He knows your time, your season, and what you are capable of handling. [Ecclesiasts 3:8]

When King David went into the war as well as Joshua and many other kings they would always inquire of God to hear if that was his heart for the nation. Those king's that were smart did not go into war without divine instructions. Today many are going into war and have no idea what we are fighting and what is coming up against us. We are so quick to take on a battle. We need to stop and think, and ask ourselves is this a battle that I should be fighting.

My dad told me that when he was young, in his early years of boxing, he took whatever fight came his way. However, later he began to choose his own fights. Every battle is not ordained for you.

The body of Christ needs to possess the spirit of discernment. We need to know what battles we are to fight and what battles we are to leave alone.

Sometimes, God just wants you to stand still and see the salvation of the Lord. There are other times when you need to be like Joshua and hear the voice of God. You need to know that He has given you your marching orders and it's time to pursue. [Joshua 8:1]

Remember, when God is sending you out, the battle is already won. You need to know who your Commander-in-Chief is and who is sending you into battle.

We need to understand Satan has no power over you unless God gives him permission. Even with that he can only operate in the boundaries of God. When you are God's He has you covered. [Job 1:10]

Understand God knows all about Satan. He is a created being. If we need to know anything just go to the Word and the Word will reveal and inform us with everything we need to know. The Word of God reveals Lucifer's tricks and tactics. God has openly exposed him. God has revealed it to his church. [Isaiah 54:16, Luke 10:18, Revelation 12:10, John 8:44]

Understand Satan is not your friend. He stands for nothing good, and no good can be found in him. He is a deceiver and wants to deceive you. Understand he was a praiser and a worshipper of God. However, pride sat in and he tried to exalt himself above God. This is a danger we must not allow pride to interfere with our purpose.

This is our opponent and we must not sleep in the same bed or live in the same house with it. Pride will have you think it is you and have you give credit and glory to yourself when glory alone belongs to God. Do not allow pride to overtake you. Pride is subtle. Pride is what got Satan kicked out of heaven and it is what kicked man out of the garden. [Ezekiel 28:17-18, Genesis 3:4-6]

Pride agenda is to have one rebel against the Word of God. It makes you think that you are not hurting anyone. But the truth is it defiles you and will destroy you if not dealt with. [Proverbs 16:8-19, I Corinthians 3:16-18]

Pride operates like it is in submission but has another agenda. It character is to usurp authority and leave you confused. One thing about pride it keeps you blind to its motives. Will make you think it is everyone else. Pride has you take the focus off of yourself and blame others. God hates when pride operates in His people. [Proverbs 8:13]

We can do nothing and are nothing without Christ. We must continually check ourselves to make sure that pride is dealt with. When you start looking for other to praise you for what you have done for the kingdom. This will open the door and allow Satan access to the rooms that are in your house. Pride will take you off your purpose and open you up for torment.

Know what you're fighting and ask hard questions concerning your the motives of our heart. Why do I want this? What is this about? Am I in this to bring glory to God or to myself? Why did I just do or say what I said? Be truthful and answer the questions honestly. Everything we do is not always lined up with the Word of God. Repent and move on, and close the door or doors. Do not allow this demon any more access. Remember in Satan dwelleth no good thing. He is the father of lies. Just like in your flesh that wants to fight to do what it wants. In your flesh there is nothing good. [Romans 7:17-18]

Throughout Scriptures when it comes to pride the Father will deal with it. Just like he dealt with Satan, Adam and Eve. The Father will grab hold of pride and cast it to the ground.

Therefore, in knowing your opponent one must know what is in them and that it is able to stand up against any demon.

The Word is greater and more powerful than any demon.
[James 4:7]

Scripture References:

Ecclesiastes 3:8 - "A time to love, and a time to hate; a time of war, and a time of peace."

Joshua 8:1 - "And The Lord said unto Joshua, Fear not, neither be thou dismayed: take all the people of war with thee, and arise, go up to Ai: see, I have given into thy hand the king of Ai and his people, and his city, and his land."

Job 1:10 - "Hast not thou made an hedge about him, and about his house, and about all that he hath on every side? thou hast blessed the work of his hands, and his substance is increased in the land".

Isaiah 54:16 - "Behold, I have created the smith that bloweth the coals in the fire, and that bringeth forth an instrument for his work; and I have created the waster to destroy."

Luke 10:18 -"And he said unto them, I beheld Satan as lightning fall from heaven"

Revelation 12:10 - "And I heard a loud voice saying in heaven, Now is come salvation, and strength, and the kingdom of our God, and the power of his Christ: for the accuser of our brethren is cast down, which accused them before our God day and night."

John 8:44 - "Ye are of your father the devil, and the lusts of your father ye will do. He was a murderer from the beginning, and abode not in the truth, because there is no truth in him. When he speaketh a lie, he speaketh of his own: for he is a liar, and the father of it."

Ezekiel 28:17-18 - "Thine heart was lifted up because of thy beauty, thou hast corrupted thy wisdom by reason of thy brightness: I will cast thee to the ground, I will lay thee before kings, that they may behold thee. Thou hast defiled thy sanctuaries by the multitude of thine iniquities, by the iniquity of thy traffick; therefore will I bring forth a fire from the midst of thee, it shall devour thee, and I will bring thee to ashes upon the earth in the sight of all them that behold thee."

Genesis 3:4-6 - "And the serpent said unto the woman, Ye shall not surely die: For God doth know that in the day ye eat thereof, then your eyes shall be opened, and ye shall be as gods, knowing good and evil. And when the woman saw that the tree was good for food, and that it was pleasant to the eyes, and a tree to be desired to make one wise, she took of the fruit thereof, and did eat, and gave also unto her husband with her; and he did eat."

Proverbs 16:18-19 - "Pride goeth before destruction, and an haughty spirit before a fall. Better it is to be of an humble spirit with the lowly, than to divide the spoil with the proud."

1 Corinthians 3:15-18 - "Know ye not that ye are the temple of God, and that the Spirit of God dwelleth in you? If any man defile the temple of God, him shall God destroy; for the temple of God is holy, which temple ye are. Let no man deceive himself. If any man among you seemeth to be wise in this world, let him become a fool, that he may be wise."

Proverbs 8:13 - "The fear of the LORD is to hate evil: pride, and arrogancy, and the evil way, and the froward mouth, do I hate."

Romans 7:17-18 - "Now then it is no more I that do it, but sin that dwelleth in me. For I know that in me (that is, in my flesh,) dwelleth no good thing: for to will is present with me; but how to perform that which is good I find not."

James 4:7 - "Submit yourselves therefore to God. Resist the devil, and he will flee from you."

CHAPTER EIGHT

DRESSING FOR WARFARE
THE ARMOUR OF GOD

"Put on the whole armour of God (not partial), that ye may be able to stand against the wiles of the devil."
Ephesians 6:11

"Able-dunamai-doo-nan-ahee- Strong's # G1410 to be able, to have power-combines power, willingness, inherent strength and action."[8]

"For we wrestle not against flesh and blood, but against princi- palities, against powers, against the rulers of the darkness of this world, against spiritual wickedness in high places." Ephesians 6:12

A dear friend of mine said to me one day, "We, the Body of Christ, need to be able to discern what's going on in the

---

[8] Jack W. Hayford, Litt.D., Bishop Ithiel C. Clemmons, M.Div.,Ph.D.,D.D.,
Spirit Filled Life Bible (KJV), 1991, 1995, Thomas Nelson Publishers.

atmosphere, and begin to pray the solution and not the problem." [Matthew 6:10]

When we are able to discern the motivating spirit behind what is trying to come against us, we will not fight each other. We need to discern the difference between spiritual struggles, as well as social, personal and political difficulties. You see, if the enemy can get you unfocused, you will be swinging at things that cannot hurt you.

If he can keep us focused on things that have no power or influence over our life, he will slide his way in and try his best to kill us. We do not wrestle against flesh and blood (each other). We wrestle against principalities, powers, rulers of the darkness of this world, and spiritual wickedness in high places.

We fight against, to name a few:

- Territorial demons that want land, power, authority and wealth.
- Witchcraft
- Dumb and deaf spirits, which come to conceal the works of other spirits that are at work. [2 Corinthians 10:3-5, Ephesians 6:13]

Again, Paul sees it very important to mention the whole armor of God.

"Withstand, anthistemi (anth-is-tay-mee); Strong's #H436: Compare "antihistamine." From anti, "against," and histemi, "to cause to stand." The verb suggests vigorously opposing, bravely resisting standing face-to-face against an adversary, standing your ground. Just as an antihistamine puts a block on histamine, anthistemi tells us that with the authority and spiritual weapons granted to us we can withstand evil forces."9

"Stand therefore, having your loins girt about with truth, and having on the breastplate of righteousness;"
Ephesians 6:14

Boxers wear a cup to protect their loins, which protects them from getting hit below the belt. This cup stays in place as long as it is tied properly. Occasionally, boxers are hit below the belt and are given warnings. If they continue, they will lose points or be dis- qualified.

As Christian warriors, we must remember Satan does not follow the rules. He always hits you below the belt every time he gets a chance. Satan does not fight fair but God always gives us a way to escape. [1 Corinthians 10:13]

When Paul talks about the armor of God, he used an example of an early first century Roman soldier's uniform. It had a belt that went around the waist, which held the other parts of the armor in place. When the soldier moved, the belt prevented the uniform from making noise, which would

---

9 Jack W. Hayford, Litt.D., Bishop lthiel C. Clemmons, M.Div.,Ph.D.,D.D., Spirit Filled Life Bible *(KN)*, 1991, 1995, Thomas Nelson Publishers.

have alerted the enemy. The belt was a stabilizer. As Christian warriors, we must come to know that the Word of God is the stabilizer.

The Word of God is the absolute truth and authority that is able to stand on its own. [John 8:32]

Truth has the ability to expose and disarm the works of the devil. Satan, on the other hand, is the father of lies. Understand when truth is at work because we are his disciples and we are His disciples because we continue in His word, John 8:33. When getting dressed know that truth is a powerful piece that you should be wearing. When you are walking and wearing truth what has had you unable to see is no more present. Your eyes are no more blinded because you choose to abide in the vine. When we are not abiding we are blind and open to any attack of the enemy. We will not know what hit us until we are on the ground and a few days later. [2 Corinthians 4:4]

When Satan moves, everything rattles and if you are in tune with the things of God, you can hear him when he is coming. [John 8:44]

Jesus came to make you free. He came to destroy the works of the devil. Satan cannot do anything to you unless God has given him permission.

The breastplate covers the soldier's most vital organ, his heart. The high priest wore a breastplate (Leviticus 8:8), and in the breast- plate, the urim and thummin were placed, which represented all the wisdom and counsel of God. The heart is protected and inside of your heart lies wisdom and the counsel of God.

*"And your feet shod with the preparation of the
gospel of peace; " Ephesians 6:15*

*"Ye, though I walk through the valley of the shadow of
death, I will fear no evil: for thou art with me; thy rod and
thy staff they comfort me." Psalm 23:4*

Proper shoes allow you to move forward in battle. It is very
important for a boxer shoes to be just right. Boxers need to
be able to move quickly in the ring, with much confidence.

*"Above all, taking the shield of faith, wherewith ye shall be
able to quench all the fiery darts of the wicked. "
Ephesians 6:16*

Boxing gloves and a boxer's reach can be considered as
their shield of faith because they can block the onslaught of
punches that their opponent is throwing at them.

I can remember my dad just sticking his jab out there, and
keeping it there, to throw the fighter's punches off. This
prevented his opponents from connecting a punch. The
opponent would become unfocused and try to use another
strategy. You need to know when to put your jab out there.
Know that it will accomplish what you intend for it to do.

The Roman soldier's shield was soaked in a special solution.
When the fiery darts came and they hit the shield, the
substance in the solution was able to extinguish the fiery
darts. We need to increase our faith by hearing the Word of
God, so when the fiery darts come our way, the anointing of
God will quench every dart that is thrown. [1 John 5:4,
Hebrews 11:1 and Romans 10:17]

The measure in which we read, hear, and obey God's word, is the measure in which faith will be released and increased in our lives.

"And take the helmet of salvation, and the sword of the Spirit, which is the word of God:" Ephesians 6:17

Protect your mind. Your mind must be fortified with the knowledge of salvation. If you are unsure of your salvation, you are not going to be effective in warfare.

The sword of the Spirit is the Word of God. It is the "logos", the written Word, and "rhema", the spoken Word. The sword can be used as an offensive weapon, as well as a defensive weapon. Using the Word of God, as the sword, is more than reading or quoting scripture-**its power!**

I know one thing about my dad's jab: it is quick, sharp, and power- ful. His jab alone can knock you out. If a jab can stop you, what do you think the Word of God can do? The Word of God will have the enemy leave you alone. [Hebrews 12]

Scripture References:

Matthew 6:10 - "Thy kingdom come. Thy will be done in earth, as it is in heaven."

2 Corinthians 10:3-5 - "For though we walk in the flesh we do not war according to the flesh: (For the weapons of our warfare are not carnal, but mighty through God to the pulling down of strongholds;) Casting down imaginations, and every high thing that exalteth itself against the knowledge of God, and bringing in captivity every thought to the obedience of Christ;"

Ephesians 6:13 - "Wherefore, take unto you the whole armour of God, that ye may be able to withstand in the evil day, and having done all, to stand."

1 Corinthians 10:13 - "There hath no temptation taken you but such as is common to man: but God is faithful, who will not suffer you to be tempted above that ye are able; but will with the temptation also make a way to escape, that ye may be able to bear it."

John 8:32 - "And ye shall know the truth, and the truth shall make you free."

2 Corinthians 4:4 - "In whom the god of this world hath blinded the minds of them which believe not, lest the light of the glorious gospel of Christ, who is the image of God, should shine unto them."

John 8:44 - "Ye are of your father the devil, and the lusts of your father ye will do. He was a murderer from the beginning, and abode not in the truth, because there is no truth in him. When he speaketh a lie, he speaketh of his own: for he is a liar, and the father of it."

1 John 5:4 - "For whatsoever is born of God overcometh the world: and this is the victory that overcometh the world, even our faith."
Hebrews 11:1 - "Now faith is the substance of things hoped for, the evidence of things not seen."

Romans 10:17 - "So then faith cometh by hearing, and hearing by the word of God."

Hebrews 4:12 - "For the word of God is quick, and powerful, and sharper than any two-edged sword, piercing even to the dividing asunder of soul and spirit, and is a discerner of the thoughts and intents of the heart."

CHAPTER NINE

GOING INTO BATTLE

My dad said that he is always prepared before he goes into
the ring. He has his music playing and he's led into the
arena. The playing of the music distracts his opponents and
gets them unfocused. They are so busy keeping their eyes
on the opponent that they are not keeping their eyes on the
prize. However, the God we serve is always focused. He
never sends you into a battle without you coming out the
victor.

*"And they rose early in the morning, and went forth into the
wilderness of Tekoa: and as they went forth, Jehoshaphat
stood and said, Hear me, O Judah, and ye inhabitants of
Jerusalem; Believe in the LORD your God, so shall ye be
established; believe his prophets, so shall ye prosper. And
when he had consulted with the people, he appointed singers
unto the LORD, and that should praise the beauty of
holiness, as they went out before the army, and to say,
Praise the LORD; for his mercy endureth for ever. And when
they began to sing and to praise, the LORD set
ambushments against the children of Ammon, Moab, and
mount Seir, which were come against Judah; and they were
smitten. For the children of Ammon and Moab stood up
against the inhabitants of mount Seir, utterly to slay and
destroy them: and when they had made an end of the
inhabitants of Seir, every one helped to destroy another. And*

*when Judah came toward the watch tower in the wilderness,
they looked unto the multitude, and, behold, they were dead
bodies fallen to the earth, and none escaped. And when
Jehoshaphat and his people came to take away the spoil of
them, they found among them in abundance both riches with
the dead bodies, and precious jewels, which they stripped off
for themselves, more than they could carry away: and they
were three days in gathering of the spoil, it was so much.
And on the fourth day they assembled themselves in the
valley of Berachah; for there they blessed the LORD:
therefore the name of the same place was called, The valley
of Berachah, unto this day. Then they returned, every man
of Judah and Jerusalem, and Jehoshaphat in the forefront of
them, to go again to Jerusalem with joy; **for the LORD
had made them to rejoice over their enemies.**" 2
Chronicles 20:20-27*

My dad does not enter into the ring without music or an
entourage. Remember, praise and worship precede every
battle. Praise and Worship disarm your opponent's artillery
and empowers you. [Psalms 100:4]

We should never go into battle without being led by the
Holy Spirit. Our Heavenly Father always prepares the way
before we enter into battle and a host of angels are
encamped about us. [Psalms 34:7]

It is very important to read the Word of God and get the
Word of God in you. So you will be equipped, prepared and
know how to use the Word of God to bring glory to God. In
doing this, it will stop the enemy in his tracks and have him
retreating in seven different directions. [Deuteronomy 28:17,
James 4:7]

Not only will God have the enemy retreat but He will make you a fenced brazen wall that the enemy will not be able to have access to you, unless you allow him. [Jeremiah 15:20]

Remember God will give you the strategy and the technique on how to take the enemy out if you inquire of Him. This is all about the preparation process if you don't hear God you don't move. [John 10:4-5, 1 Samuel 30:8, 1 Chronicles 14:10-16]

My natural dad never leads himself into the ring. He is always being lead by someone he can trust. He has his arm on the person in front of him and he is relying on them as his guide. His *entourage* and security team surrounds him in order to protect him from the onslaught of spectators that are trying to get at him which would distract him from his assignment.

Satan and his army are the spectators in our lives. They are looking for any act of disobedience as an entrance into our lives. Thanks to God, there is a hiding place for those who are in Christ Jesus. [Psalms 32:7]

"He that dwelleth in the secret place (hiding place) of the most High shall abide under the shadow of the Almighty."
Psalm 91:1

"Dwelleth- ya"shab -yaw-shab'); Strong's #H3427: A primitive root; properly to sit down (specifically as judge, in ambush, in quiet); by implication to dwell, to remain; causatively to settle, to marry: - (make to) abide (-ing), continue, (cause to, make to) dwell (-ing), ease self, endure, establish, habitation, (make to) inhabit (-ant), make to keep [house], lurking, X marry (-ing), (bring again to) place, remain, return, seat, set (-tle), (down-) sit (-down, still, - ting down, -ting [place] -uate), take tarry."[10]

"I will say of the LORD, He is my refuge and my fortress: my God; in him will I trust."Psalm 91:2

"Refuge- machseh -makh-as-eh', makh-seh'; Strong's H4268; from H2620; a shelter (literally or figuratively): - hope, (place of) refuge, shelter, trust."[11]

"Surely he shall deliver (snatch away, set free) thee.from the snare of the fowler, and from the noisome pestilence. He shall cover thee with his feathers, and under his wings shalt thou trust: his truth shall be thy shield and buckler. Thou shalt not be afraid for the terror by night; nor for the arrow that lieth by day; Nor for the pestilence that walketh in darkeness; nor for the destruction that wasteth at noonday. A thousand shall fall at thy side, and ten thousand at thy right hand; but it shall not come nigh thee. (Can't touch you) Only with thine eyes shalt thou behold and see the reward of the wicked. Because thou hast made the LORD, which is my refuge, even the most High, thy habitation; There shall no evil befall thee, neither shall any plague come nigh thy dwelling."
Psalm 91:3-10

"Habitation- maw-ohn', maw-een'; Strong's # H4583; from the same as H5772; an abode, of God (the Tabernacle

---

[10] James Strong, LL.D.,S.T.D. The New Strong's Exhaustive Concordance of the Bible, 1822-1894, Thomas Nelson Publishers, 1990.

[11]J ames Strong, LL.D.,S.T.D. The New Strong's Exhaustive Concordance of the Bible, 1822-1894, Thomas Nelson Publishers, 1990.

or the Temple), men (their home) or animals (their lair); hence a retreat (asylum): - den, dwelling ([-]) place), habitation."[12]

"For he shall give his angels charge over thee, to keep thee in all thy ways. They shall bear thee up in their hands, lest thou dash thy foot against a stone. Thou shalt tread upon the lion and adder: the young lion and the dragon shalt thou trample under feet. Because he hath set his love upon me, therefore will I deliver him: I will set him on high, because he hath known my name. He shall call upon me, and I will answer him: I will be with him in trouble; I will I will deliver him, and honour him. With long life will I satisfy him, and show him my salvation.
"Psalms 91:11-16

Scripture References:

Psalms 100:4 - "Enter into his gates with thanksgiving, and into his courts with praise: be thankful unto him, and bless his name."

Psalms 34:7 - "The angel of the LORD encampeth round about them that fear him, and delivereth them."

Deuteronomy 28:7 - "The LORD shall cause thine enemies that rise up against thee to be smitten before thy face: they shall come out against thee one way, and flee before thee seven ways."

---

[12] James Strong, LL.D.,S.T.D. The New Strongs's Exhaustive Concordance of the Bible, 1822-1894, Thomas Nelson Publishers, 1990.

James 4:7 - "Submit yourselves therefore to God. Resist the devil, and he will flee from you".

Jeremiah 15:20 - "And I will make thee unto this people a fenced brasen wall: and they shall fight against thee, but they shall not prevail against thee: for I am with thee to save thee and to deliver thee, saith the LORD."

John 10:4-5 - "And when he putteth forth his own sheep, he goeth before them, and the sheep follow him: for they know his voice. And a stranger will they not follow, but will flee from him: for they know not the voice of strangers

1 Samuel 30:8 - "And David enquired at the LORD, saying, Shall I pursue after this troop? shall I overtake them? And he answered him, Pursue: for thou shalt surely overtake them, and without fail recover all."

1 Chronicles 14:10-15 - "And David enquired of God, saying, Shall I go up against the Philistines? and wilt thou deliver them into mine hand? And the LORD said unto him, Go up; for I will deliver them into thine hand. So they came up to Baalperazim; and David smote them there. Then David said, God hath broken in upon mine enemies by mine hand like the breaking forth of waters: therefore they called the name of that place Baalperazim. And when they had left their gods there, David gave a commandment, and they were burned with fire. And the Philistines yet again spread themselves abroad in the valley. Therefore David enquired again of God; and God said unto him, Go not up after them; turn away from them, and come upon them over against the mulberry trees. And it shall be, when thou shalt hear a sound of going in the tops of the mulberry trees, that then thou shalt go out to battle: for God is gone forth before thee to smite the host of the Philistines. David therefore did as God commanded him: and they smote the host of the Philistines from Gibeon even to Gazer."

Psalms 32:7 - "Thou art my hiding place; thou shalt preserve me from trouble; thou shalt compass me about with songs of deliverance. Selah."

CHAPTER TEN

A RETURN

As my dad continued to share his experiences with me, he said, "Every time I fight, I expect a return." There's always a payment coming after the fight. In fact, he receives a down payment on the fight before he even fights.

We should expect a return when we go into battle. The return should be salvation, deliverance, healing, prosperity, etc. For example, when the children of Israel were ordained by God to go into battle, many times they received the spoils of the land.

He also informed me that, before he was educated on every aspect of boxing, he did not realize that you could receive profits from film rites. Every time they show his fights, someone is being paid. He said, even when he is gone, someone will still be paid.

However, with the knowledge that he has received, he benefits from the film rights. You need to leave an inheritance for your children's children.

The Scripture says:

"A good man leaveth an inheritance to his children's children: and the wealth of the sinner is laid up for the just."
Proverbs 13:22

When the children of Israel went into war they always had a return. The principle of God is that when you do His will blessing will always be a part of your life. [Genesis 14:14-16, 2 Chronicles 20:22-25]

It is important to know when you do what God tells you to do even when it comes to taking your position in war that victory is always on the other side and there is a payment. The enemy has to drop everything He has held that belongs to you. [Deuteronomy 28:7]

Also, understand when we go to war we always find the enemy trying to steal something that belongs to us. It's time for us to get paid. [Proverbs 6:31]

Don't allow the enemy to steal anymore. It's time to know that God has given you rights. If you do not know your rights do not expect the enemy just to hand it over. When we accepted Christ we now have become heirs and joint heirs. God is a good God and is faithful to those who love, trust and believe on him. Come out of the doubt and watch the Word of God work for you as we do damage to the Kingdom of darkness. We are more than conquerors in Christ Jesus.

Scripture References:

Genesis 14;14-16 - "And when Abram heard that his brother was taken captive, he armed his trained servants, born in his own house, three hundred and eighteen, and pursued them unto Dan. And he divided himself against them, he and his servants, by night, and smote them, and pursued them unto Hobah, which is on the left hand of Damascus. And he brought back all the goods, and also brought again his brother Lot, and his goods, and the women also, and the people."

2 Chronicles 20:22-25 - *"And when they began to sing and to praise, the LORD set ambushments against the children of Ammon, Moab, and mount Seir, which were come against Judah; and they were smitten. For the children of Ammon and Moab stood up against the inhabitants of mount Seir, utterly to slay and destroy them: and when they had made an end of the inhabitants of Seir, every one helped to destroy another. And when Judah came toward the watch tower in the wilderness, they looked unto the multitude, and, behold, they were dead bodies fallen to the earth, and none escaped. And when Jehoshaphat and his people came to take away the spoil of them, they found among them in abundance both riches with the dead bodies, and precious jewels, which they stripped off for themselves, more than they could carry away: and they were three days in gathering of the spoil, it was so much."*

Deuteronomy 28:7 - *"The LORD shall cause thine enemies that rise up against thee to be smitten before thy face: they shall come out against thee one way, and flee before thee seven ways."*

Proverbs 6:31 - *"But if he be found, he shall restore sevenfold; he shall give all the substance of his house."*

CHAPTER ELEVEN

TAKING A PUNCH

On March 25, 1978, in Las Vegas, Earnie Shavers delivered the hardest punch that my dad has ever taken. "Earnie Shavers gave you a lot to think about. Mainly it came to his punching power. Of all the fighters I ever fought, nobody could punch harder. Not Tyson, not Gerry Cooney, not Ken Norton. Shavers' punches numbed your bones. Those other guys hit hard. When they landed, their punches hurt. But Shavers was in a league all his own. Shavers was, as Jerry Izenberg once described him, "a right-hand puncher who could hit you in the neck and break your ankle."[13]

I can remember that fight as if it was yesterday. My dad was winning the fight, and during the seventh round, Ernie Shavers hit my dad and he went down. Later, my dad informed me that he took a blow to the head. As he was on the canvas, I can remember my sister Lisa and I saying," Daddy get up, Daddy get up." Then we heard the voice of the crowd on television chanting;"Lar-ry, Lar-ry, Lar-ry", and he got up and won that fight.

---

[13] Larry Holmes, Phil Berger, Larry Holmes: Against The Odds, 1998, St Martin's Press, New York, 96.

There are going to be times when you're going to fall but it is what you do when you're down. Remember that you have the Greater One living in you, reminding you who you are and telling you to get up. In addition, you have a host of angels in your comer calling your name and encouraging you. We were lying on our backs too long. It is time to get up and be counted instead lying down and being counted out. [1 Corinthians 15:58]

With God on your side and fighting your battles, the one that is defeated is Satan. [Isaiah 54:7}

You need to remember that, the very weapon that is formed against you in battle, God made it. [Isaiah 54:16]

The devil can't bring anything your way without God knowing the potential of the weapon that he's trying to use against you.

Because of our position and our seat in Christ Jesus, we know that we are more than conquerors. Remember, greater is He that is in you, than he that is in the world.

My dad got up off that ring, and fought that fight. He won by unanimous decision by remembering who he was, and what was put in him. You can't keep a good man down.

We need to understand that Jesus is sitting on the right hand of God making intercession for us. He is telling us that the battle has already been won because he has conquered death, hell and the grave.

If Satan could not hold Christ in the grave, what makes you think that he has the power or the authority to hold you in yours? You are no longer in bondage because you are in Christ and Christ is in you. Christ has opened up your grave and its time for you to get up, walk out of it and claim what belongs to you. Hallelujah!

Don't allow things in your past to keep you from obtaining the prize. God has some great things in store for you. If you choose to stay in the grave, with darkness devouring you, you will never be able to see the light. Jesus is saying, "My child, come forth." [Matthew 18:18, 1 John 3:8]

Christ has commissioned us to go into the world. [Mark 1615-18]

You need to know that, if the greater One is living on the inside of us and He is complete, then that means that we are also complete in Christ Jesus. God has already equipped us with everything we need. It's up to us to use what He has already given us. No weapon that the enemy throws our way can prosper because we are established, set in the righteousness of God. This makes us a glorious people, waiting for the Father to say, "Well done!" Face to face.

Scripture References:

1 Corinthians 15;58 - "Therefore, my beloved brethren, be ye steadfast, unmovable, always abounding in the work of the Lord, forasmuch as ye know that your labour is not in vain in the Lord"

Isaiah 54:17 - "No weapon that is formed against thee shall prosper; and every tongue that shall rise against thee in judgment thou shalt condemn. This is the heritage of the servants of the LORD, and their righteousness is of me, saith the LORD."

Isaiah 54:16 - "Behold, I have created the smith that bloweth the coals in the fire, and that bringeth forth an instrument for his work; and I have created the waster to destroy"

All power has been given unto him in heaven and in earth. "Matthew 28:18

1 John 3:8 - "....For this purpose the Son of God was manifested, that he might destroy the works of the devil."

Mark 16:15-18 - "And he said unto them, Go ye into all the world, and preach the gospel to every creature. He that believeth and is baptized shall be saved; but he that believeth not shall be damned. And these signs shall follow them that believe: In my name shall they cast out devils; they shall speak with new tongue; They shall take up serpents; and if they drink any deadly thing. It shall not hurt them; they shall lay hands on the sick, and they shall recover."

CHAPTER TWELVE

CONCLUSION

I pray that, after reading this book, you have gained an insight on how to stand against the battles that will come into your life.

For your spiritual growth and development, I have compiled a list of Scriptures to empower you on your Christian journey. In order to effectively survive the storms of life, you need to know Who You Are In Christ, What You Have In Christ and What You Can Do In Christ.

May the blessings of the Lord come upon you and overtake you.

The Prize Fight

Prayer of Salvation

You read this book and may want to accept Jesus Christ as your personal Savior. If so, then pray this prayer with me:

Dear Jesus, I ask that you come into my life and forgive me of my sins. I acknowledge that the wages of sin is death; but the gift of God is eternal life through Jesus Christ our Lord. For your word says that knowing Christ Jesus is eternal life. You said in your word, "that if I shall confess with my mouth that the Lord Jesus, and shall believe in my heart that God, has raised him from the dead, I shall be saved." Well Jesus, I make this confession today that you are the only begotten Son of God and He has raised you from the dead. I believe in you, Jesus, and your birth, death, burial, and resurrection, and you are seated on the right hand of the Father making intercession for me. Thank you, Jesus, for coming into my life and saving me. I pray this in Jesus name. Amen!

Prayer of Rededication

Father, I come to you, as I know that I am a backslider, and I would like to rededicate my life back to Christ. I acknowledge my sins and "that the wages of sin is death; but the gift of God is eternal life through Jesus Christ." I know that Jesus is the Son of God and, without Him in my life, there is eternal damnation. I rededicate my life back to you, along with everything that is in me. I give you my gifts and my talents. In Jesus name I pray. Amen!

The Prize Fight

Who You Are In Christ

Romans 8:16 – Children of God
Romans 8:17-Joint Heirs with Christ
Roman 8:37-More than Conquerors
I Corinthians 3:16 – Temple of God
I Corinthians 6:15 -Members of Christ
I Corinthians 6:19-Temple of the Holy Spirit
II Corinthians 5:17-New creature
II Corinthians 5:21 – Righteousness of God
II Corinthians 6:16-Temple of the Living God
II Corinthians 6:18-Sons and daughters
Galatians 3:29-Heirs of Promise
Ephesians 2:10-God's workmanship
Ephesians 1:19 -Greatness of power
Ephesians 5:29-32 -Church, His body
Colossians 1:12-Saints in light
Colossians 2:10-complete
I John 3:2 – sons
I Peter 2:9-Chosen generation, royal priesthood,
holy nation, peculiar people
Revelations 1:6 – Kings and priests

What You Have In Christ

Proverbs 3:1-2,8,10,13,15-18,24-26-Length of days, peace,
health, plenty, happiness, wisdom, understanding, riches,
honor, life, sweet sleep, pleasantness, lack of fear,
confidence
Isaiah 53:4-Lack of grief (worry)
Isaiah 53:5-Forgiveness of sins, peace and health
Luke 10:19-All power over the enemy
Matthew 8:17 - Lack of sickness
Romans 12:3 -Measure of faith
I Corinthians 2:16 – The mind of Christ

Galatians 2:20-Faith of Son of God
Ephesians 3:12 – Boldness, confidence of faith
Ephesians 4:7-Grace (everyone)
Philippians 4:19 - All my needs met
Colossians 1:27-Christ in you, the hope of Glory
II Timothy 1:7-Power, love, sound mind
I John 2:27-Anointing
Romans 12:3 – Measure of faith

What You Can Do In Christ

Matthew 16:19-Bind and loose in earth
Mark 16:17 -cast out devils
Mark 16:18 -take up serpents (not to go looking for them)
drink deadly things and not be hurt (not purposely, do not
mock God) lay hands on sick and they recover.
John 14:12-Do works of Jesus
John 14:14-Ask anything in his name
John 17:22-Be one with Jesus
John 17:26-Love as Jesus loved
Romans 8:9-Be in the Spirit
Romans 10:8-Preach the word of faith
I Corinthians 2:15 -Be spiritual and judge all things
James 5 :14-15 -Pray, prayers of faith Lord will raise up and
forgive sins
I John 4:4-Overcome the world

BIBLIOGRAPHY

Schultz, Samuel J. *Broadening Your Biblical Horizons, Old Testament Survey, Part I: Genesis-Ester.* 7. Print.

Hayford, J Jack, and Bishop Ithiel C. Clemmons. *Spirit Filled Life Bible (KJV),.* Thomas Nelson, 1991-1995. Print.

Evans, Anthony T. *Winning the Invisible Battle.* Urban Alternative, 1991. Print.Alternative, Inc., 4.

Purpose | Define Purpose at Dictionary.com." *Dictionary.com | Find the Meanings and Definitions of Words at Dictionary.com.* Web. 26 Sept. 2011. <http://dictionary.reference.com/browse/purpose>.

Purpose. (1995). In *Strong's exhaustive concordance: King James.* (Updated ed.). Retrieved September 26, 2011, from http://www.biblestudytools.com/concordances/strongs-exhaustive-concordance/

Berger, Phil. *Against The Odds.* By Larry Holmes. New York: St. Martin's, 1998. 96. Print.

Strong, James, LL.D.,S.T.D. The New Strong's Exhaustive Concordance of the Bible, 1822-1894, Thomas Nelson Publishers, 1990.

ABOUT THE AUTHOR

Pastor Misty along with her husband Pastor Jeffrey Dorsey is the pastors of Revival Fire Ministries International, in Easton, Pennsylvania. They have three children Jason Rheinert, Jeffrey Jr. and Jessica Chapman and one son-in-law Maurice Chapman and seven grandchildren. Pastor Misty Dorsey is the daughter of the Former Heavyweight Champion Larry Holmes and Amelia Bowles of Easton, Pennsylvania.

God has given her a mandate to birth an end-time prophetic ministry that operates under the anointing and power of the Holy Spirit. She gave birth to Revival Fire Ministries, Inc. on June 6, 2004 under the leadership of Pastor Marcella Jordan. Pastor Roslyn Durham of The Sword of the Lord Churches International is her pastor and overseer.

Pastor Misty has traveled abroad and has ministered in Israel, Liberia, West Africa, Ghana, West Africa, Malawi, Southern Africa, Amsterdam, Western Netherlands, Dominican Republic, Commonwealth of Dominica, Haiti, Bermuda and White Mountain Apache "Canyon Day Lighthouse Family Church" in Arizona, as well as many states in the U.S.

Pastor Misty has birth Revival Fire Ministries – Easton, Allentown/Bethlehem, Pottstown all of PA and Staten Island, NY. Also, Pastor Misty oversees Prophet Maude McCullough & Pastor Larry McCullough of the Fathers Embrace in Philadelphia, PA and Pastor Lisa Salazar, La Vina Verdadera de Dios Internacional in Poconos, PA, Prophet Tiffany Webster with Intimacy with Christ Ministries, Poconos, Pennsylvania and Reverend Carolyn Carter with Great Adonai Ministries in Bowie, Maryland.

Pastor Jeffrey and Pastor Misty oversee two churches in West Africa one in Seniagya, Ashanti-Ghana and one in Intumkoso. Also, and three churches in Malawi, South Africa in Blantyre Chilimba and in Ntcheu Ntonda and in Thyolo and one church in Mozambique.

She is founder of School of Prophets/Seers in Easton, Allentown/Bethlehem, Pottstown, Poconos all of PA, Staten Island, Brooklyn both of New York. She is one of the co founders and the visionary of Revival Fire School of Ministries a minister of Revival Fire Ministries, Inc. a ministry affiliated with Faith Bible College out of Missouri.

*Pastor Misty is also the author of **The Prize Fight**, **Principles for Ministry** and **Book of Joshua 40 Day Daily Devotional**. She is a former social. Pastor Misty is in ministry full-time.*

Her desire is that the Word of God will go forth like a two edge sword throughout the world and spare not, and call the people into repentance so they may be saved, delivered, set free, and live a spirit-filled victorious life that Christ has promised.

But whoever takes a drink of the water that I will give Him shall never, no never, be thirsty anymore. But the water that I will give him shall become a spring of water welling up (flowing, bubbling) [continually] within him unto (into, for) eternal life. John 4:14 (Amplified)

You can contact Misty or find out more about her and her other ministry materials at www.mistyholmesdorsey.com, You can also follow Misty on her Facebook fan page at www. https://www.facebook.com/mistyholmesdorsey.

The Prize Fight

57042678R00056

Made in the USA
Middletown, DE
28 July 2019